MULTIPOLARITY

ALL OVER THE PLACE

ANURAAG BHATTACHARYA

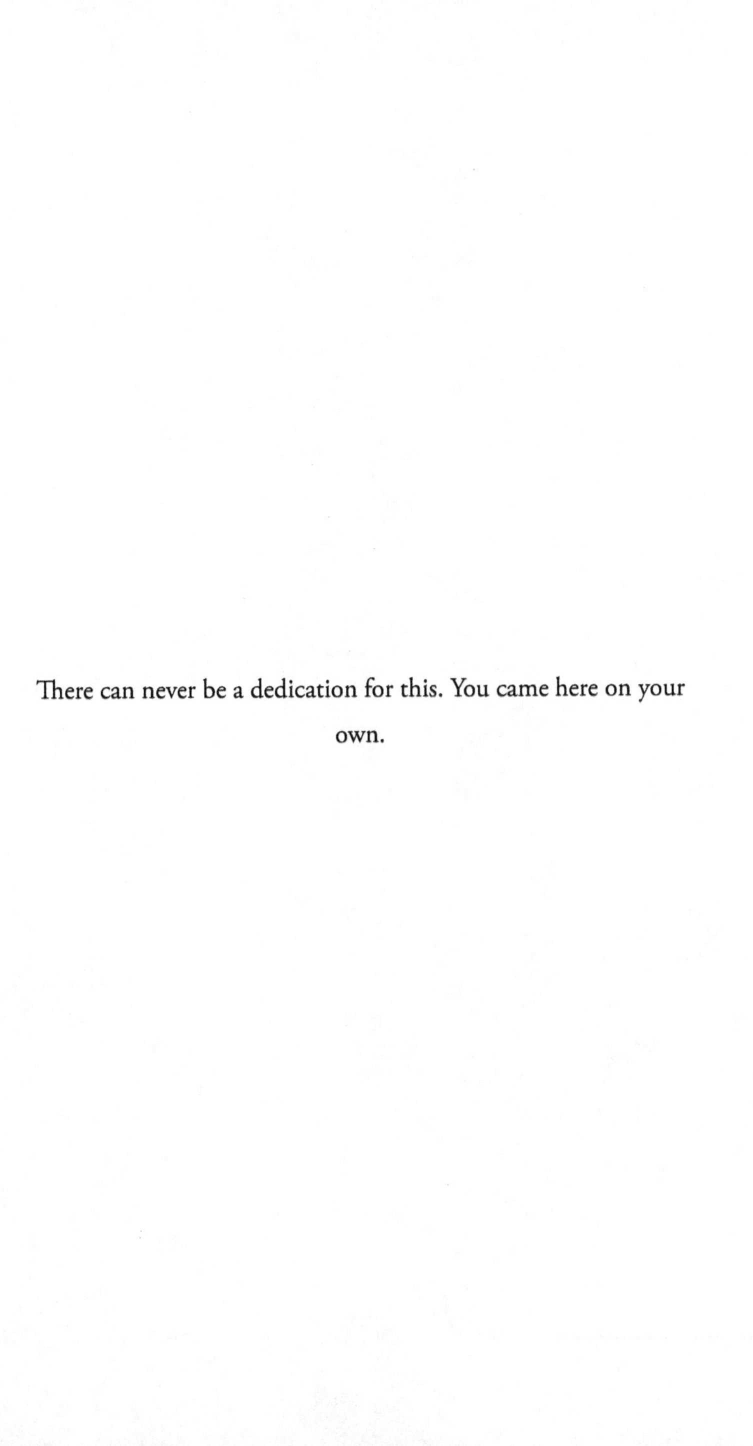

There can never be a dedication for this. You came here on your own.

Contents

Preface

Where do I begin? At this point this feels more like a formality. All I can say is, suit yourself!

Do you remember where you've been last summer? I do, and I do remember the summer that precedes that. Being able to remember is a curse. That has been my lesson from this summer.

- 12th October, 2022

1. Little kitty!

My little kitty,

my soft ball of fur,

purring your way to my heart,

you're one who knows,

when I need the love,

when I need the snuggle,

when I need the bed,

with someone to hold.

My little kitty,

this is a shame,

that you don't have all these years that I do,

even if they say you have nine lives,

you will be gone before I know,

And honestly,

that is what I envy,

you are always there for me,

but I don't want you to be here forever.

This world has never deserved you,

this place never even knew,

the value of love that you bring to the table,

the gift of kindess when she put on a sable,

the people, they never cared,

but I do, I promise, my little kitty.

They came, and they left,

while they said shit about you,

they jumped on the fence,

and took over the lawn,

with their head so dense,

but you stayed still, and did what you do the best.

My little kitty,

you are here for me, I know,

but when the time comes, I will let you go.

2. Walk of Shame!

Never gave a thought before giving in,
such a blunder,
such a shame,
such disasters for petty fame!
The tricky design,
the maze of deception,
the lies placed in a line,
wrapped around me like a venom pine.
You seem to have taken the devil's vow,
how do you act so pure, "so holy than thou?"
I was walking the line,
engrossed in the shame,
when I knew I was just another pawn,
in that bizarre game.
I kept up as far as I could,
I pulled through as long as I should,
now if you need me again,
your search ends in vain,
as I will disappaear,
vanish in thin air,
now don't come running, crying that's not fair.
In case, if you want to know,
I am just fine,

in my corner, in my safe place,

I am never coming out,

never to that cruel face.

3. What's real and what's not?

The questions run like bouncing balls,
striking the walls of my mind
like the sadist manaics,
hitting my weaker spots.
Hell may have witnessed the fall,
the rise and then the fall again.
With the fearsome tone,
the devils chide,
"if you had taken the time out,
to look back and wonder,
that was the spot that you missed.
Now when you're so far on the road,
only a fool would stop
and stay undecided.
So tread ahead,
and finish what you started,
as only the cowards abandon,
in the midst of it all."
Million other thoughts,
with million other realities,
tying the possibilities,
of what could and what could not,

sipping on that funny tasting concoction,

of the joys and the sorrows.

As I pull up on the highway,

and watch them move past,

I wonder what they left behind,

and what they would go after,

after leaving behind what they have been reaching towards.

4. silent scream/cruel kindness

In the world of allusion,
you seem to thrive,
in the deep sea of sanctimony,
when you take the dive.
Go ahead!
There's no shame!
I wonder how much did you gain,
when you put it on sale,
in return for the soul,
of those who never questioned,
of those who never doubted,
of those who never ill-willed,
of those who never bothered,
for themselves.
The people like you,
the kind that you are,
are the ones who I resent,
the perfect examples,
for the object of indignation,
for the hate,
that you fill me with,
for that you'll never be forgiven.

Hope I can forget,
hope I never remember,
the one that you were,
the one that you are,
hope I never come across,
the one that you will become,
for I have my peace,
I won't sell it to you,
and when you don't get your way,
you try to snatch it away.
Thus, I hope,
you stay in that pit forever,
and never come around,
just never, ever!

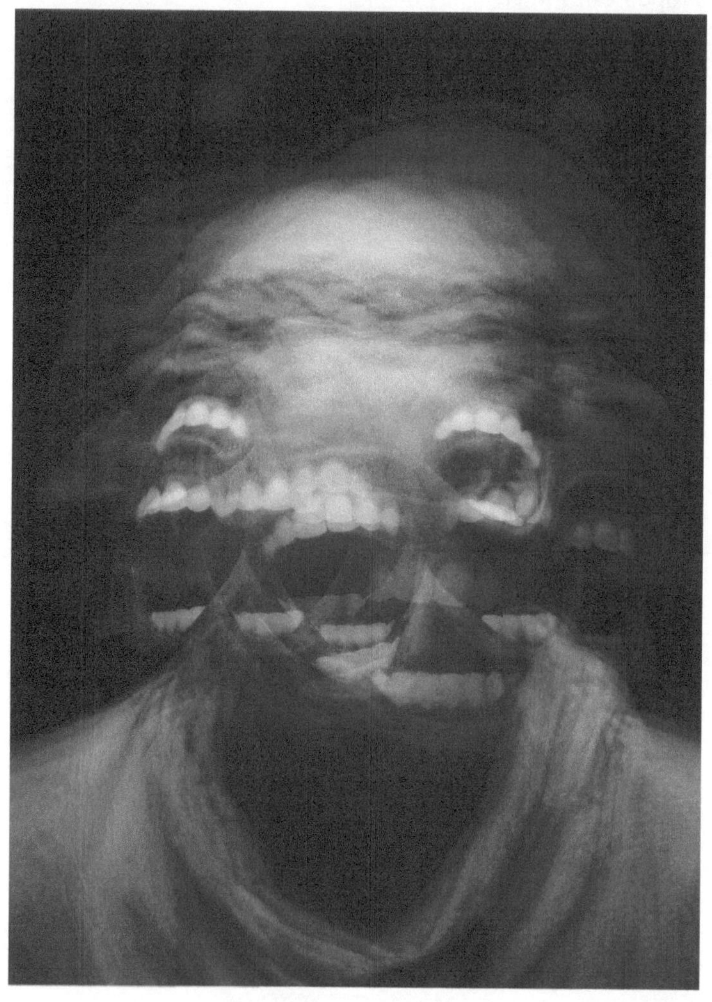

5. pictures and grabs

Those objects, those moments,
once precious,
have seemed to lose their value overnight!
Those kind gestures,
those loving words,
have been rendered useless over time!
Those pictures,
the polaroids, the digital grabs,
are just some stream of ink and pixels,
never can they be of any need anymore!
Objects hold their place,
as long as they desired,
once they are regular,
they have no charm,
you get them for you are driven,
by greed, by lust, by hunger,
once satiated,
they are as good as garbage!
Fortunate for the fact,
destiny is never bored,
someone else's garbage becomes a treasure,
overnight!
For them who are driven by fresh desires,

of hunger, greed and lust,

for them they remain special,

till they turn into garbage and then treasure.

And there it goes!

6. Gone in the air!

The broken records,
the burnt photographs,
the torn scarves,
the bug infested books,
the overgrown garden weed,
the beloved pet buried in the backyard,
the lost diamond heirloom,
the stolen rubies,
the mossy paintings,
the forgotten recipes,
the vanishing lingo,
the dysfunctional television set,
the dead telephone,
the rotting furnitures,
the dampened walls,
the banisters falling apart,
the house, decaying and still standing tall.
The diminished strength,
the failing will,
the fading beauty,
the bending spine,
the wealth looted,
the health, giving up.

The impermanence,

the everlasting sadness,

the faint joyful memories,

the forever emptiness.

7. Multipolarity - All over the place

Who ever cared?
And who did not?
For the chords that tied,
from depth of the soul,
to the ones that got your heart full.
Now how does that feel?
When the wires got ripped apart,
for there was a load that was off?
The slience has been here for long.
What got missed in between?
What got left out, did you see?
I know the answer,
you work hard for those you value,
and those who you don't, lose it for you,
and your ego gets popped like a balloon,
when you poke a pin with a slight strike,
only thing is, its you who hand it over,
the pin, I am saying.
They call it a connection,
there has to be a circuit,
somewhere, the wires are apart, they need repair.
How soon do you do it, that decides the age,

the age and value of what you had but you didn't see.
Reality is different, with million different possibilities,
which one you choose, is upto you.
You get it sometime, and sometimes you don't.
Or else its too late, too late to bother,
too late to start over.
Time never waits, so why would you ?

8. missing piece of the puzzle

The petals are wilted,
the pawn was not on the chess board,
the cassettes dont play anymore,
the photographs are lost somewhere,
they are not in my memory,
on repeat played Taylor's Evermore.
I was in the hopes,
when they dashed down,'
crashed hard on the surface,
except I who still lived.
I thought it was silly,
silly beyond the silliness,
of my hopes and my dreams,
the reason felt unreasonable for a while.
So I was still for a second or two maybe,
I don't really remember.

9. Connecting.... Ringing....
Declined.... Unconnected!

I heard that you left some things unsaid,

and some things haven't been said to you,

and that is why,

you spend so many nights,

without catching any wink,

like the star studded sky,

talks to you in the lowly whispers,

and they ask you, how long do I have to see you like this?

And one fine hour,

you try to find them again,

in the memories,

thanks to tech and that cloud,

what you see looks so real.

Is it something that you think that you missed,

while you were busy syncing them into the memories?

You see,

and you wonder,

so many questions seek their answer,

and that is why you pick it up,

you dial their name!

What do you find at 3AM?
The phone rings just for 30 seconds,
"The numer you're trying to reach isn't answering at the moment.
Please try after sometime!"
So when the 'after sometime' passes by,
you try again,
you hear two rings,
and "the number you're trying to reach is currently busy,
please try after sometime!"
That's a decline, and that's an answer.
Not for the questions that's for sure,
but for you to hear and learn.
You go back to the memories in the cloud,
the night sky, thus gives a silent sigh,
so you turn around,
the connection is now disconnected.

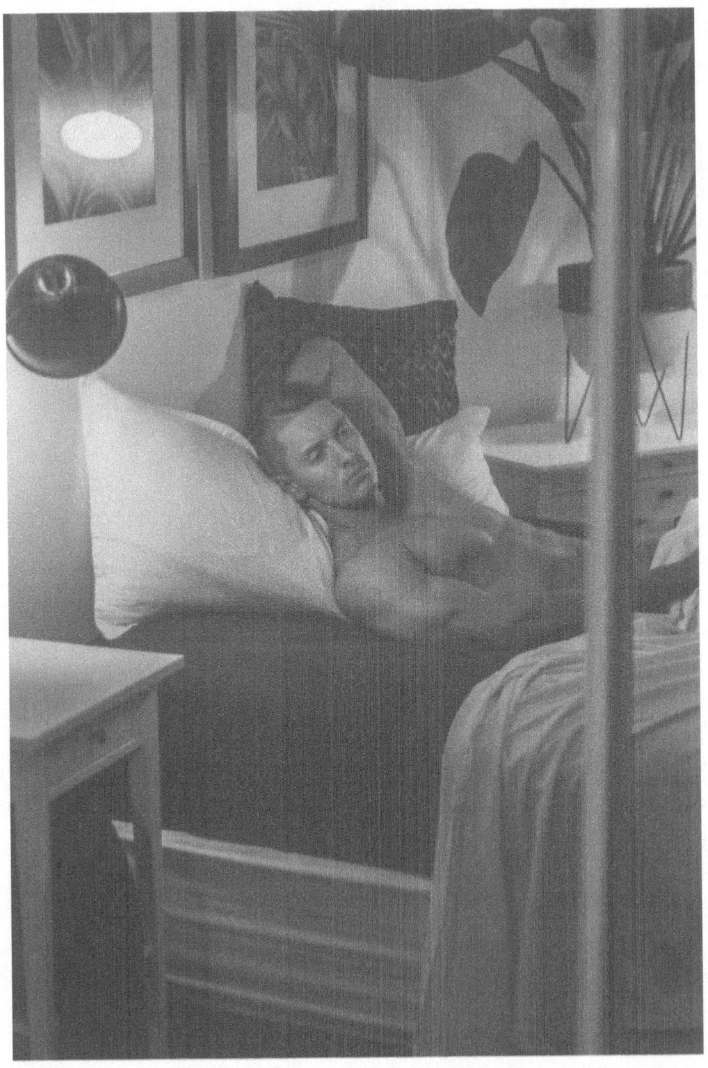

10. Night is lonely sitting at the bar

No, the night isn't lonely,

but what is,

is the one who you carried,

by the bar table,

you see that pretty girl dancing under the ball,

she looks lovely in the star light,

wearing her bright blue dress,

she lives in that moment,

that moment is all for her,

and underneath it all you see,

she carries what you do,

what you did in the bar this night,

there is this stud, with his glass of on the rocks,

what trouble does he get bothered with, you wonder,

you look into his eyes, they're intense,

his salt and pepper is screaming,

so is his suit and leather shoes,

he is so handsome, his heart is sore,

so sore, it shows up in his face,

he does, and that is why you know,

he carries what you carry,

the night you see,

will be lonely again when they leave,

this bar you see will lose them in a while,

the bartenders thus, do their job,

and leave for their solace,

where they do not take with them,

what the bar carries,

that woman and that gentleman,

and what you carry.

11. Madness of Intent

The morning before I intended,
to pull the strings apart,
so the life will never overflow,
and the air would never pass through,
I went to see the sunrise,
as a mortal for the last time.
That morning when I intended,
I made myself a breakfast,
with my favourite drink,
four shot espresso by the side,
I wanted to stop,
and I wanted to shine,
and then I thought,
I would be living the same reason,
step on the same mines,
over and over,
and die a hundred times,
while I breathe.
That morning as I intended,
I saw how to tie a knot,
over the video stream,
yes, that morning I was sure that I intended,
to stop me from doing what I was doing,

and as I did what I intended to do,

I wished my father was gone before me,

just like my mother did.

And you might want to call it selfish,

but I was the most unselfish I have ever been.

I was not lucky, I couldn't do,

what I intended,

the madness of the moment,

was clear, a few minutes, and it would have been done for sure.

12. Song from the grave

I hope you will come and listen,
while I sing from my grave,
the song that you loved to listen,
which I sang for you,
while I was there with you.
The song with the tune,
the words that you loved so much,
the voice was a sweet nectar,
overflowing through the jar,
the song will stay through the worlds,
through the windows you must peek,
and you can hear the faint little sounds,
for a moment and you'll realise,
oh they stayed.
The song stayed.
My song that stayed.

SuperCDing 90
B